Zeus

BY VIRGINIA LOH-HAGAN

Gods and goddesses were the main characters of myths. Myths are traditional stories from ancient cultures. Storytellers answered questions about the world by creating exciting explanations. People thought myths were true. Myths explained the unexplainable. They helped people make sense of human behavior and nature. Today, we use science to explain the world. But people still love myths. Myths may not be literally true. But they have meaning. They tell us something about our history and culture.

45th Parallel Press

Published in the United States of America by Cherry Lake Publishing
Ann Arbor, Michigan
www.cherrylakepublishing.com

Content Adviser: Matthew Wellenbach, Catholic Memorial School, West Roxbury, MA
Reading Adviser: Marla Conn MS, Ed., Literacy specialist, Read-Ability, Inc.
Book Designer: Jen Wahi

Photo Credits: © HildaWeges Photography, 5; © 4Max/Shutterstock.com, 6; © Ataly/Shutterstock.com, 8; © Sara Robinson/Shutterstock.com, 11; © Artepics Alamy Stock Photo, 13; © Howard David Johnson, 2016, 15; © Vuk Kostic/Shutterstock.com, 17; © rudall30/Shutterstock.com, 19; © villorejo/Shutterstock.com, 21; © Rose Hayes/Shutterstock.com. 22; © Chronicle/Alamy Stock Photo, 25; © fluke samed/Shutterstock.com. 27; © World History Archive/Alamy Stock Photo, 29; © Howard David Johnson, 2016, Cover; various art elements throughout, shutterstock.com

45th Parallel Press is an imprint of Cherry Lake Publishing.

Library of Congress Cataloging-in-Publication Data

Names: Loh-Hagan, Virginia, author.
Title: Zeus / by Virginia Loh-Hagan.
Description: Ann Arbor : Cherry Lake Publishing, [2017] | Series: Gods and goddesses of the ancient world | Includes bibliographical references and index.
Identifiers: LCCN 2016031181| ISBN 9781634721318 (hardcover) | ISBN 9781634722636 (pbk.) | ISBN 9781634721974 (pdf) | ISBN 9781634723299 (ebook)
Subjects: LCSH: Zeus (Greek deity)--Juvenile literature. | Gods, Greek--Juvenile literature. | Mythology, Greek--Juvenile literature.
Classification: LCC BL820.J8 L65 2017 | DDC 292.2/113--dc23
LC record available at https://lccn.loc.gov/2016031181

Printed in the United States of America
Corporate Graphics

ABOUT THE AUTHOR:

Dr. Virginia Loh-Hagan is an author, university professor, former classroom teacher, and curriculum designer. She would love to be king of the gods. She'd command the gods to bring her yummy food all day long. She lives in San Diego with her very tall husband and very naughty dogs. To learn more about her, visit www.virginialoh.com.

TABLE OF CONTENTS

CHAPTER 1

KING OF GODS

Who is Zeus? How was he born? Who did he marry?

Zeus was a Greek god. He was the king of the 12 **Olympians**. These gods were the rulers of the gods. They lived on Mount Olympus. Mount Olympus is in Greece. It's the highest mountain in Greece.

Zeus's parents were Cronus and Rhea. Zeus was the youngest child. His parents were **Titans**. Titans were giant gods. They ruled until the Olympians took over.

Cronus was told that a son would take away his power. So, Cronus ate his children. Rhea saved Zeus. She hid Zeus in a cave. She tricked Cronus. She wrapped a rock in baby clothes. She gave Cronus the rock instead.

Zeus hid at Crete. Goddesses and goats raised him. The goddesses clashed their swords. This hid the sound of Zeus crying.

Zeus grew up. He tricked Cronus. He poisoned him. Cronus threw up his children. His children were born again. So, this made Zeus the oldest child. Zeus led a war against the Titans. He and his **siblings** won. Siblings are brothers and sisters.

Zeus had long, curly hair. He had a beard.

Zeus is also called the Cloud-Gatherer.

They divided the world into three main parts. The three most powerful Olympians ruled them. Zeus was the god of the sky. Hades was the god of the underworld. Poseidon was the god of the seas. They were brothers. They fought for power.

Zeus lived on Mount Olympus. He sat on a golden throne. He looked upon the world. He saw everything. He ruled over all.

Zeus married his sister, Hera. Hera was the goddess of women and marriage. She didn't like him at first. Zeus changed shape. He disguised himself as a cuckoo bird.

Family Tree

Grandparents: Uranus (Father Sky) and Gaia (Mother Earth)

Parents: Cronus (god of time) and Rhea (goddess of fertility)

Brothers: Poseidon (god of the sea), Hades (god of the underworld)

Sisters: Hera (goddess of women and marriage), Demeter (goddess of the harvest), Hestia (goddess of the hearth and family)

Spouse: Hera

Children with Hera: Ares (god of war), Eileithyia (goddess of childbirth), Hebe (goddess of youth), Hephaestus (god of fire and craftsmen)

Hera felt sorry for the bird. She took care of the bird. Then, Zeus took his true form. He made her marry him.

Zeus and Hera weren't happy. They fought a lot. Zeus had many lovers. He loved other goddesses and **mortals**. Mortals are humans. He had many children with different women.

Hera was really jealous. She did evil things. So did Zeus. Zeus protected Hera. But he didn't let anyone else love her.

Zeus fell in love easily.

CHAPTER 2

LAW AND ORDER

How did Zeus rule? What are Zeus' good deeds?

Zeus was the god of sky, lightning, thunder, law, order, and justice. He was the most powerful god.

He ruled over the gods. He made sure gods did their jobs. He punished them for bad behavior.

He ruled over mortals. He watched over them. He tried to make their lives fair. He oversaw their destinies. He had two jars of **fate**. Fate is the things that happen to a person. The jars were at his feet. One jar had bad things. One jar had good things. He gave out both good and bad fate. He rewarded people for good deeds. He punished them for bad deeds.

He kept track of time. He determined the time of a mortal's death. He changed the seasons. He controlled day and night.

Zeus was the "Great Punisher." He enforced laws. He didn't like liars. He didn't like **oathbreakers**. These are people who break their promises. He would strike them with lightning. This was his greatest power.

Zeus has golden scales.

All in the Family

Zeus had many children. His favorite was Heracles. Heracles's mother was a mortal. Her name was Alcmene. Hera was jealous. She sent two snakes to kill Heracles. Heracles was in his crib. He choked the snakes. Hera also tried to drown Heracles in a storm. Zeus punished her. He hung her upside down from the sky. But that didn't stop her. Hera drove Heracles crazy. Heracles killed his wife and children. The gods got mad. They punished Heracles. Heracles had to perform 12 labors. Labors are heroic tasks. For example, he had to slay Hydra. Hydra was a dragon with many heads. Heracles was the greatest Greek hero. He was the strongest human. He was stronger than many gods. He became a god when he died. He was given a home on Mount Olympus. He was given a goddess for his wife.

As punishment, Zeus made Sisyphus roll a rock up a hill.

Phineus could see the future. Phineus gave away Zeus's secrets. Zeus punished him. He blinded him. He put him on an island. He put food in front of him. But monsters took away the food. Zeus let him starve.

Sisyphus tricked people. He was cruel. In one story, Zeus punished him. He made him roll a huge rock up a mountain. The rock would roll down. Sisyphus had to roll the rock up again. He had to do this forever.

Zeus was a peacemaker. Gods fought a lot. Zeus solved their fights.

Apollo and Hermes were gods, and half brothers. Hermes stole Apollo's oxen. Apollo was angry. Hermes denied stealing the oxen. But Zeus made him tell the truth. Finally, Hermes and Apollo made a trade. Hermes killed a cow. He killed a tortoise. He stretched the cow guts across the empty tortoise shell. This was the first **lyre**. A lyre is a musical instrument. Hermes played the lyre. He entranced Apollo. So Apollo traded his oxen for music.

Asclepius tried to raise the dead. This upset Hades. Hades was in charge of the dead. Zeus punished Asclepius. He killed him with lightning.

 Zeus loved to laugh. He was wise. He tried to be fair and just.

CHAPTER 3

STRIKING LIGHTNING

What were some of Zeus' powers? What were his bad deeds?

Zeus was the most powerful god. He controlled all the gods' powers. He could remove or give powers. Many gods feared him. They didn't defy him. They tricked him instead. Zeus was also **unpredictable**. Nobody could guess his decisions. He got mad easily. He hit people with lightning. He did this whenever he wanted.

He controlled weather. He controlled the movements of the stars, sun, and moon. He could make total darkness. He could make good weather. He could make bad weather. He flooded out people when he was mad. He caused storms when he was mad.

Zeus didn't like to be tricked. But he tricked others. He could copy people's voices. He could sound like anyone. He could change shapes. He could look like an animal or a person. He tricked many of his lovers this way.

He would also turn people into animals. He did this as punishment. Zeus visited King Lycaon. The king didn't

Zeus got mad easily, and hit people with lightning.

Real World Connection

Zeus must have been really mad at Roy Sullivan. Sullivan was a park ranger. He worked in Shenandoah National Park in Virginia. He had a world record. He was hit by lightning seven times. He was called "Spark Ranger" and "Human Lightning Rod." Strike one happened while hiding in a tower. It burned his right leg. Strike two happened while driving. It took off his eyebrows and eyelashes. Strike three happened while gardening. It knocked him out. Strike four happened while working. It set him on fire. Strike five happened while driving. It knocked off his shoe. Strike six happened while walking on a trail. Strike seven happened while fishing. It burned him. It caused hearing loss. People didn't want to stand next to him. They were afraid of getting struck. He died at age 71, but not from lightning. The odds of getting hit by lightning seven times are 4.15 in 100,000,000,000,000,000, 000,000,000,000,000.

Zeus changed King Lycaon into a wolf.

believe it was Zeus. He fed Zeus human flesh. Zeus got mad. He punished the king. He turned the king into a wolf. Lycaon may have been the first werewolf.

CHAPTER 4

THROWING THUNDERBOLTS

What are Zeus' weapons? What are his symbols?
Who are his servants?

While fighting the Titans, Zeus and his brothers saved
the **Cyclopes**. Cyclopes were giants. They had one eye.
They were imprisoned. They were grateful to be released.
They gave each brother a weapon. Hades chose a helmet
of darkness. Poseidon chose a **trident**. Tridents are spears.
Zeus chose a thunderbolt.

The thunderbolt was Zeus's most powerful weapon.
He loaned the thunderbolt to Athena. Athena was the
goddess of wisdom. Zeus's most famous power was his

ability to throw thunderbolts. He had a winged horse named Pegasus. Pegasus carried the thunderbolts for Zeus. An eagle retrieved the thunderbolts.

The thunderbolt cut off mountains. It destroyed islands. It boiled water. It destroyed cities. It killed people and defeated gods.

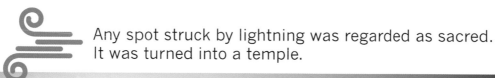
Any spot struck by lightning was regarded as sacred. It was turned into a temple.

Zeus's symbols are the thunderbolt, eagle, bull, and oak tree.

Aetos Dios was a giant golden eagle. It served Zeus. It sent messages. It kept Zeus company. It used to be a mortal king. The king was worshipped like a god. That made Zeus mad. Zeus turned him into an eagle. Zeus liked eagles. Eagles fly high in the sky. They're as fast as lightning.

Zeus changed into eagles a lot. He also changed into bulls. Zeus wanted Europa. He changed into a white bull. He hung out with the herd. Europa saw the bull. She petted it. She rode it. Then, Zeus took her to the sea. He took her to the island called Crete. She became the first queen of Crete.

Cross-Cultural Connection

Indra was an Indian god. He was the king of gods. He was the god of war. He was the god of heavens. He was the god of the sun. He was the god of rain and storms. He had a lightning bolt. He slayed a sea monster. The sea monster ate all the water. It caused a drought. Indra killed it with his thunderbolt. Clouds had heavenly cows. Demons tried to steal these cows. Indra fought the demons. Thunder was the sound of them fighting. Indra milked the cows. This was rain. Indra protected cows. He had a magical ax. He shaped mountains and valleys. He created rivers and streams. He lived on Mount Meru in the clouds. He pushed up the sky. He released dawn from a cave. He was a great warrior. He had a golden body, jaw, nails, hair, and beard. He rode a golden cart. He had four arms.

Zeus had a special shield. He wore it on his chest. The shield was called aegis. It was awful to look at. It killed anyone who saw it. It turned others to stone. It was an animal skin. It had a gold surface. It had scales. It had a monster head. It inspired fear. When Zeus shook it, thunder rolled.

Harpies were the "**hounds** of Zeus." Hounds are like dogs. They did Zeus's dirty work. They are the monsters who tortured Phineus. They bothered mortals. They kidnapped mortals. They had wings. They were women. They had ugly faces. They had bird bodies.

 Zeus's harpies lived on the island of Crete.

Harpyia

25

CHAPTER 5

BEWARE OF THE SKY-GOD

What are some stories about Zeus?

There are many myths about Zeus.

One is that Zeus gave birth. He was married before Hera. He married a Titan named Metis. Metis helped him trick Cronus. Metis didn't like Zeus at first. She changed forms. She hid. Zeus won her over. Metis became pregnant. A goddess told Zeus that their child would kill him. So, Zeus swallowed Metis. He didn't want her to give birth. Metis's baby grew inside of Zeus's head. Zeus got a headache. Another god used a golden ax. He split Zeus's head open. Out came Athena. Athena was his daughter. Zeus gave her the aegis.

Zeus wanted to fill the earth with mortals. He asked Prometheus to create mortals. Prometheus created them from clay. He based their bodies on the gods. He gave them minds. He wanted to protect them. He asked Zeus to give them some fire. Mount Olympus had sacred fire. Zeus said

Zeus didn't want to give fire to mortals.

no. Prometheus didn't listen. He took fire. He hid it in straw. He gave it to mortals.

This made Zeus mad. Zeus chained Prometheus to a mountain. Zeus had an eagle eat Prometheus's liver. Zeus

Explained By Science

Ancient Greeks thought an angry Zeus threw bolts down to earth. Science has a different explanation. Lightning is a sudden release of electricity. It's made by thunderclouds. Thunderclouds have many bits of ice. These frozen raindrops move around. They bump into each other. These bumps create an electrical charge. Clouds fill up with electrical charges. Positive charges form at the top of clouds. Negative charges form at the bottom. Opposite charges attract. Positive charges build up from the ground. They collect around something that sticks up from the ground. They connect with charges coming from clouds. Then, lightning strikes. It's six times hotter than the sun's surface. Lightning can happen inside clouds, between clouds, and from clouds to the ground.

Zeus didn't like it when things were stolen from him.

healed the liver overnight. The next day, the eagle would eat it again.

Don't anger the gods. Zeus had great powers. And he knew how to use them.

DID YOU KNOW?

- There was a temple at Olympia. It honored Zeus. The townspeople hosted games every four years. They did this to entertain and honor Zeus. The games were called the Olympic Games.

- Zeus's greatest enemy was Typhon. Typhon was strong. The Olympians ran away from him. Zeus fought him. Typhon ripped away Zeus's muscles. Zeus became weak. Another god helped Zeus to regain his strength. Zeus fought Typhon again. He trapped him under Mount Etna. Typhon became a volcano.

- Zeus turned ants into an army.

- Zeus's main shrine was in Dodona. There were holy oak trees there. The wind blew through the leaves. People believed the wind told the future.

- Zeus had four guards. They were spirits. They had wings. Their names were Kratos (Strength), Zelos (Rivalry), Nike (Victory), and Bia (Force).

- Mnemosyne was the goddess of memory. She was one of Zeus's lovers. They had nine children. The children are the Muses.

- Zeus kidnapped a human boy named Ganymede. He took him to Mount Olympus. He made him immortal. Immortal means living forever. Ganymede served as his cup-bearer.

CONSIDER THIS!

TAKE A POSITION Read the other 45th Parallel Press books about the Greek gods. Which god do you think should be the king of gods? Was Zeus the right choice? Argue your point with reasons and evidence.

SAY WHAT? Reread Chapter 5. Summarize the myths about Zeus. Explain what the myths tell us about Zeus's character.

THINK ABOUT IT! Zeus was the god of justice. He gave out punishments. Read about some of Zeus's punishments. Did his punishments fit the crime? Do you think his punishments were fair or unfair?

LEARN MORE

Nardo, Don. *Zeus*. Hockessin, DE: Mitchell Lane Publishers, 2015.

O'Connor, George. *Zeus: King of the Gods*. New York. First Second, 2010.

Temple, Teri, and Robert Squier (illustrator). *Zeus: King of the Gods, God of Sky and Storms*. North Mankato, MN: Child's World, 2012.

Wilbur, Helen L., and Victor Juhasz (illustrator). *Z is for Zeus: A Greek Mythology Alphabet*. Ann Arbor, MI: Sleeping Bear Press, 2008.

GLOSSARY

Cyclopes (SYE-klop-eez) giants with one eye

fate (FAYT) the things that happen to a person

hounds (HOUNDZ) vicious dogs

lyre (LIRE) a stringed musical instrument like a harp

mortals (MOR-tuhlz) humans

oathbreakers (OHTH-brayk-urz) people who break promises

Olympians (uh-LIM-pee-uhnz) rulers of the gods who live on Mount Olympus

siblings (SIB-lingz) brothers and sisters

Titans (TYE-tunz) giant gods who ruled before the Olympians

trident (TRYE-dent) three-pronged spear

unpredictable (uhn-prih-DIK-tuh-buhl) behaving in a way that is not expected

INDEX